THE WISDOM OF
ANCIENT GREECE

Compiled by Jacques Lacarrière
Photographs by Jacques Lacarrière

Abbeville Press   Publishers
New York   London   Paris

To Caroline, for her Kore-like smile

Cover illustration and vignettes by Danielle Siegelbaum

For the English-language edition
RESEARCH, TRANSLATION FROM THE FRENCH, AND BIBLIOGRAPHY:
John O'Toole
EDITOR: Jacqueline Decter
TYPOGRAPHIC DESIGN: Virginia Pope
PRODUCTION EDITOR: Owen Dugan

For the original edition
SERIES EDITORS: Marc de Smedt and Michel Piquemal
DESIGNER: Dominique Guillaumin

First edition
10 9 8 7 6 5 4 3 2 1

Library of Congress Cataloging-in-Publication Data

Paroles de la Grèce antique. English.
The wisdom of ancient Greece/compiled by Jacques Lacarrière;
photos. by Jacques Lacarrière.
p. cm.
Includes bibliographical references.
ISBN 0-7892-0243-3
1. Quotations, Greek—Translations into English. I. Lacarrière,
Jacques, 1925–   . II. Title.
PN6080.P1613 1996
089'.81—dc20   96-17066

For well over a thousand years ancient Greece literally teemed with wise men, from the ninth century B.C. when the poet Homer was active, until the fateful year A.D. 530, when the Christian emperor Justinian closed the Academy of Athens and forbade the teaching of pagan philosophy. We might argue that Greece, along with India, was the land that boasted the greatest number of sages per square mile. There were wise men of every type, appearance, and caliber. There were those who, like Empedocles, would declaim their works while walking about the agora and city streets dressed in sumptuous tunics and crowned with headbands like prophets. Others, like Plato, would teach wisely seated on the tiered steps of the Academy, or at least on the shaded slope of a hill. Still others, like Aristotle, would walk up and down the paths and gardens of the Lyceum followed by their disciples, hence their nickname, peripatetics, literally those who pace to and fro, strollers. Finally, there were those who, like Diogenes and the Cynics, would sleep right in the streets, living on alms and dispensing their teaching to one and all while wearing rags rather than the *himation*, a cloak typically worn by philosophers that betokened nobility of the blood and the soul.

There were indeed thousands of wise men and philosophers in ancient Greece, some at the head of academies, authors of important and acknowledged works; others practically unknown, even anonymous, who have left us but a few fragments collected by some compiler or later historian. Wisdom, *sophia* as the Greeks called it (and still call it today), was an integral part of philosophy, which in turn could not be dissociated from social and collective life. Thus the reader will find in this collection, gleaned from among a dozen or so ancient authors, remarks and observations that stem not from a single, revealed truth—as would be the case several centuries later in Christianized Greece—but rather from questions, intellectual quests, a continuous and manifold investigation of the world. In a word, they represent incertitudes as much as certitudes. It is in precisely this way that the wisdom of ancient Greece remains vital today. Whereas certain wise men like Plato propose a precise and coherent system of thought, others like Democritus, Epicurus, Diogenes, and Pyrrho, the so-called Materialists, Cynics, and Skeptics, offer quite varied and personal answers. The ancient Greeks endlessly questioned the world, and because that world gave them no precise answer, let alone a sole and unique response, each school and each century provided its own in often quite vivid turns of phrase.

Moreover, wisdom is found not only among the wise, or at least among those who profess to be so. From time to time it crops up where one least expects it, on the tomb of a slave, for instance, in a popular proverb, or in a poem by Sappho, Greece's earliest yet most unforgettable poetess. We should bear in mind that for the Greeks wisdom was incarnated not in a god, but rather in a goddess, Athena.

By ranging over the schools and the centuries then, we will discover in fables, maxims, sayings, and prayers the myriad aspects of Greek wisdom, so vast and open that more than one path is needed to reach it.

Jacques Lacarrière

Know thyself.

Inscription on the Temple
of Apollo in Delphi
(sixth century B.C.)

Charioteer, Delphi (c. 475 B.C.)

Time is a child playing at draughts,

a child's kingdom.

Heraclitus, fragment LXXIX
(sixth century B.C.)

May God grant me love for that which has splendor;

but in this time of my life let me strive for attainable things.

Pindar, *Pythian Odes* 11
(fifth century B.C.)

Only the gods can never age, the gods can never die. All else in the world almighty Time obliterates, crushes all to nothing. The earth's strength wastes away, the strength of a man's body wastes and dies— faith dies, and bad faith comes to life, and the same wind of friendship cannot blow forever, holding steady and strong between two friends, much less between two cities. For some of us soon, for others later, joy turns to hate and back again to love.

Sophocles, *Oedipus at Colonus*
(fifth century B.C.)

The Oaks presented a complaint to Jupiter, saying, "We bear for no purpose the burden of life, as of all the trees that grow we are the most continually in peril of the axe."

Jupiter made answer, "You have only to thank yourselves for the misfortunes to which you are exposed: for if you did not make such excellent pillars and posts, and prove yourselves so serviceable to the carpenters and the farmers, the axe would not so frequently be laid to your roots."

Aesop
(probably sixth century B.C.)

Some say a host of cavalry, others of infantry, and others of ships, is the most beautiful thing on the black earth, but I say it is whatsoever a person loves.

Sappho
(sixth century B.C.)

Kore, or young girl, Acropolis, Athens (sixth century B.C.)

Alive,
I was a man among the men of this world.
Dead,
I am the equal of Darius* in the mystery.

Inscription on a slave's tomb
(fourth century B.C.)

*Persian king famous for his wealth and immense empire.

There is a marvel here such as I know not by fame on Asian ground, or as ever born in the great Dorian isle of Pelops—a growth unconquered, self-renewing, a terror to the spears of enemies, a growth which mightily flourishes in this land—the gray-leafed olive, nurturer of children.

Sophocles, *Oedipus at Colonus*
(fifth century B.C.)

As to the gods, I have no means of knowing either that they exist or that they do not exist. For many are the obstacles that impede knowledge, both the obscurity of the question and the shortness of human life.

Protagoras
(fifth century B.C.)
Diogenes Laertius' *Life of Protagoras*

If you do not hope,

you will not win that which is not hoped for,

since it is unattainable and inaccessible.

Heraclitus, fragment VII
(sixth century B.C.)

At the entrance to the resting place of the Dead you shall find a source on the left. Near it stands a white cypress. Do not approach this source. You shall see another that issues from the Lake of Memory. Cool water springs forth. Guardians protect it. Say to them, "I am a child of the Earth and the starry Heavens, from whom I come, mark my words well. I am consumed and tormented by thirst. Ah, give me the cool water that springs from the Lake of Memory!" And they shall allow you to drink from the divine source, and thereafter you shall be a hero, and shall reign without end.

Orphian funeral prayer
(second century B.C.)

Wonders are many, and none is more wonderful than man; the power that crosses the white sea, driven by the stormy south-wind, making a path under surges that threaten to engulf him; and Earth, the eldest of the gods, the immortal, the unwearied, he wears away, turning the soil with the offspring of horses, as the ploughs go to and fro from year to year.

And the lighthearted race of birds, and the tribes of savage beasts, and the sea-brood of the deep, he snares in the meshes of his woven toils. …And he masters by his arts the beast…which roams the hills; he tames the shaggy-maned horse, he puts the yoke upon its neck, he tames the tireless mountain bull.

And speech, and wind-swift thought, and all the moods that mold a state, he has taught himself; and how to flee the darts of the frost, when it is hard lodging under the clear sky, and of the rushing rain....Only against Death shall he call for aid in vain; but from baffling maladies he hath devised escapes.

Cunning beyond fancy's dream is the fertile skill which brings him, now to evil, now to good. When he honors the laws of the land, and that justice which he hath sworn by the gods to uphold, proudly stands his city: no city has he who...dwells with sin.

Sophocles, *Antigone*
(fifth century B.C.)

Man is but a dream of a shadow.

Pindar, *Pythian Odes* 8
(fifth century B.C.)

When he was advised to go in pursuit of his runaway slave, Diogenes replied, "It would be absurd if Manes can live without Diogenes, but Diogenes cannot get on without Manes."

Diogenes the Cynic
(fourth century B.C.)
Diogenes Laertius' *Life of Diogenes*

There was a time when with the rest of the happy band...we beheld the beatific vision and were initiated into a mystery which may be truly called most blessed, celebrated by us in our state of innocence, before we had any experience of evils to come, when we were admitted to the sight of apparitions innocent and simple and calm and happy, which we beheld shining in pure light, pure ourselves and not yet enshrined in that living tomb which we carry about, now that we are imprisoned in the body, like an oyster in his shell.

Plato, *Phaedrus*
(fifth century B.C.)

The wisest of the wise

will never make

a crab walk straight.

Aristophanes, *Peace*
(fifth century B.C.)

When someone inquired, "Have you no concern in your native land?" "Gently," Anaxagoras replied, "I am greatly concerned with my fatherland," and pointed to the sky.

Anaxagoras
(third century B.C.)
Diogenes Laertius' *Life of Anaxagoras*

I am a pine tree broken by the wind on land.

Why do you send me to the sea,

a spar shipwrecked before sailing?

Palantine anthology
(third century B.C.)

Corinth, where are your walls, your fortresses,
Your palaces, your gardens, your pride?
Where are your handsome young men and tender maidens?
Where do your thousands of inhabitants sleep now?

War's horrible rage has laid it all low;
Nothing remains of your scattered riches;
And alone, gray nymph wandering the beach,
The gull seems to weep for the past.

Palatine anthology
(first century B.C.)

Two travelers, worn out by the heat of the summer's sun, laid themselves down at noon under the wide-spreading branches of a plane tree. As they rested under its shade, one of the travelers said to the other, "What a singularly useless tree is the plane! It bears no fruit, and is not the least service to man." The plane tree, interrupting him, said, "You ungrateful fellow! Do you, while receiving benefits from me, and resting under my shade, dare to describe me as useless and unprofitable?"

Some men despise their best blessings.

Aesop
(probably sixth century B.C.)

Men forget where the way leads….

And what they meet with every day

seems strange to them….

We should not act and speak

like men asleep.

Heraclitus, fragment V
(sixth century B.C.)

Born in 1925, Jacques Lacarrière took a degree in classical literature at the Sorbonne before leaving his native France in 1950 on what was to become a twenty-year voyage throughout Greece and the Middle East. These years abroad gave rise to several works on Greece, Egypt, and Turkey, as well as a number of French translations of ancient and modern Greek authors. And Mr. Lacarrière's travels are far from over for his next book will relate the wanderings of a mystic Sufi monk throughout Anatolia.

All of the photographs in the present collection were taken by the author in Greece over the past thirty years, except for the following:

Endpapers: *Archaic Kore*, sixth century B.C., Athens (Giraudon); *Charioteer* (detail), Museum of Delphi (© Fratelli Alinari/Giraudon, Anderson/Giraudon); *Archaic Kore*, Parthenon, Athens, sixth century B.C., (Giraudon); *Diogenes*, Rome, first–third century A.D. (Alinari/Giraudon); "The Four Seasons," Spain, third century A.D. (Lauros/Giraudon).

All the literature, philosophy and history of ancient Greece and Rome is published in the Loeb Classical Library, a series of bilingual editions offering a good English translation that rarely strays from the original text printed on the facing page.

The occasionally formal English of the Loeb translations, with its reliable and ready retinue of faithful archaisms, may not be to every reader's taste, however. For ancient Greek philosophy, a number of other translations and editions exist, especially of the works of Plato and Aristotle. We might mention here the Great Books in Philosophy series published by Prometheus Books (Amherst, New Jersey), or, from a different approach, the Texts in the History of Political Thought series brought out by Cambridge University Press. Penguin Classics also offers a panoply of the classic Greek writers in affordable paperback editions.

For a very enjoyable introduction to Greek philosophers from Thales to Epicurus written by a contemporary of the ancient world, readers would do well to dip into Diogenes Laertius' *Lives of Eminent Philosophers*, tr. R. D. Hicks, in the Loeb Classical Library (Cambridge: Harvard University Press, 1966).

As the author took care to point out in his introduction, the wisdom of ancient Greece is found not only among the writings of her philosophers, but also in the works of her poets and playwrights, in popular sayings and epitaphs. The list of translations in inexpensive editions of Homer, Pindar, Sappho, Aeschylus, Sophocles, Euripides, Aristophanes, and others is far too long to include here. However, there is one collection of verse especially worth singling out for its great compass, a bilingual anthology (with prose translations in English) that follows the history of Greek poetry to the very present: *The Penguin Book of Greek Verse*, Constantine A. Trypanis, ed. (New York: Penguin, 1971).

Several collections of or general approaches to Greek thinkers:

Barnes, Jonathan, ed. *Early Greek Philosophy*. New York: Penguin, 1987.

Bremmer, Jan N. *The Early Greek Concept of the Soul*. Princeton: Princeton University Press, 1983.

Brumbaugh, Robert S. *The Philosophers of Greece*. Albany: State University of New York Press, 1981.

Cornford, F. M. *From Religion to Philosophy, A Study in the Origins of Western Speculation*. Princeton: Princeton University Press, 1991 (reprint).

Saunders, Jason L. *Greek and Roman Philosophy after Aristotle*. New York: Free Press, 1966.